An Introduction
to the
Celtic Orthodox Church

Revised Edition

An Introduction to the Celtic Orthodox Church

Revised Edition

Fr Leonard Hollands

Lamorna Publications

Lamorna Publications
Yew Tree Studio, Marshwood, Dorset DT6 5QF

First published September 2013
This revised edition March 2022

ISBN: 978-0-9933898-6-3

Set in 11pt Verdana

Celtic Orthodox Monastery of the Holy Presence, Saint-Dolay

Contents

Illustrations

Introduction

This book is not offered as a work of theological erudition, but rather, as a simple and brief overview of Orthodox Faith, the Celtic Orthodox Church and Celtic spirituality for those beginning to explore these areas. It is hoped that this may lead to further reading. However, the best way to understand the Celtic way of worship is to experience it, and to pray it.

In the section on the Orthodox Faith I am deeply indebted to Metropolitan Kallistos Ware. Indeed, in many instances what I have written are but paraphrases of parts of his Orthodox classics *The Orthodox Church* and *The Orthodox Way.* Because I have collected prayers from various sources over the years, without noting what those sources were, I cannot, in the case of contemporary Celtic material, acknowledge the authors. For this I apologise and trust that, given the nature of the book, I shall be forgiven for any infringements of copyright.

May God bless you on your journey.

Fr Leonard

Dorset 2022

The Faith of the Orthodox Church

Before considering the Celtic Orthodox Church itself, the subject of this book, it is important to understand the Orthodox Church and its Faith in its totality. Let us, therefore, begin with a brief outline of some of the aspects which define the Faith of the Orthodox Church. This Faith is common to all jurisdictions of the Orthodox Church (setting aside the variant views of the two Natures of Christ* which exist between the Eastern and Oriental Orthodox Churches – a ridiculous nominate distinction, since Eastern and Oriental basically mean the same thing! More of this issue at the end of this section.

To be clear, then, when we refer to Greek Orthodox, Russian Orthodox, Serbian Orthodox, Celtic Orthodox and so on, we are making a distinction of ethnicity and tradition, *not* a different set of doctrines!

And so, to some key facets of the Orthodox Faith.

Tradition is greatly valued in the Orthodox Church. The Bible (Septuagint version of the Old Testament), the Nicene Creed, and the Seven* Ecumenical Councils of the Church are paramount within Tradition. Tradition holds scripture, theology and mysticism together.

Icons play an important part in Orthodoxy. They are not simply religious pictures. They are our window into the spiritual world. They are reverenced for what they represent, not as works of art, or things to be worshipped in their own right. We treat the icon *as* what it portrays.

The Orthodox Faith is strongly **Trinitarian**. God as Trinity is not an abstract theory, but is of living practical importance.

God is transcendent – above and beyond all things – and also immanent – present in His Creation. Transcendence leads us to the way of negation (apophatic theology) – what we cannot know: God is beyond our comprehension. Yet this is balanced with what we *do* know: God is Good, God is Love, etc. God's *essence* is unknowable, but His *energies* touch us.

God is *one* in essence, *three* persons. God the *Father* unbegotten from all eternity; God the *Son* begotten before all time; God the *Holy Spirit* Who proceeds from the Father (John 25.26 "the Spirit of Truth who proceeds from the Father"). The Father is the *sole* source or *arche* within the Trinity, holding it together. To proceed from the Father *and* the Son confuses the source and demotes the Holy Spirit, placing Him at the end of a line.

The Orthodox put great stress on the work of the Holy Spirit. The aim of the Christian life should be the acquisition of the Holy Spirit. Hence the frequent use of a prayer addressed to the Spirit:

> O Heavenly King, the Comforter, Spirit of Truth, You are everywhere and fill all things; Treasury of blessings and Giver of Life, come and abide in

us, and cleanse us from every impurity, and save our souls, O Good One.

The Holy Spirit is present in the Church's worship and sacraments – most notably in the *epiclesis* in the Liturgy when the Holy Spirit is invoked to make Christ present in the holy gifts.

And what of **Us**? We are made in God's image, having rationality and freedom. (The accounts of our creation in Genesis are *religious* truths, 'symbolic,' not literal history.) In what way are we made in God's likeness? We assimilate to God through virtue *so* we are *made* in His image and *called* to be in His likeness.

So, we are partakers of the Divine Nature. The aim of the Christian Life is *deification* – St Peter's second letter: "through these promises you may become partakers of the Divine Nature." (1.4) This union, however, is with God's energies, *not* His essence. *Theosis* – Deification – is the ideal that all Christians are aspiring to through life in the Church and the sacraments. Life with good works will be deified.

Thus, our **Bodies** are the temple of the Holy Spirit. The great reverence of relics comes from this high theology of the body.

Grace and **Freewill** work together. Made in His image we have freewill. Through the grace of God we are helped, but we must co-operate. That co-operation is called *Synergy*. We are, as Saintt Paul says, "fellow workers" with God. But the co-operation is unequal. God does immeasurably more than we. Our Lady is the supreme example of synergy.

The **Fall** and **Original Sin** – the Orthodox view of Adam's fall and its consequences is not as harsh as in the Latin West, which declares all humanity totally depraved and incapable of any good. Orthodox belief is that the image of God within us is *distorted* not destroyed. Humans after the fall still have free will and can choose to do good as well as evil. But sin has put a barrier between us and God. We cannot go to Him, so He comes to us.

So, the **Incarnation** is an act of God's loving kindness towards us. Christ God becomes man to offer us salvation. Christ – true God, true man; one Person, two Natures.* Fully God, fully man, in one indivisible Person. The Trinitarian revelation at Christ's *Baptism* and His *Transfiguration,* along with His *Resurrection* assure us of and focus on the Divine reality of the true Christ. His Baptism (Theophany), Transfiguration and Resurrection are, therefore, all major Orthodox feasts.

The **Crucifixion** must be seen as an entity with the Resurrection. The cross is the sign of victory (compare the Latin *Stabat Mater* with no single reference to the Resurrection).

The **Mother of God** is of great importance in the Orthodox Faith. She is given the title *Theotokos* – God bearer – usually rendered Mother of God. Mary is the most exalted among God's creatures. But she is venerated because of her relationship to Christ, and the title Theotokos was confirmed by the Third Ecumenical Council (Ephesus), *not* to exalt Mary, but to ensure the correct doctrine of Christ – that He was truly Divine in His Incarnation. It was to correct the heresy of Nestorianism, whose adherents would have preferred Christotokos, that is to say, that Mary bore only the human Nature of Christ and not the *whole* Christ.

When the Orthodox refer to Mary as "His all immaculate and all blameless holy Mother," immaculate, or spotless (*adirantos*), does not imply the Roman doctrine of immaculate conception. That would detract from her being 'one of us,' and inclines to separate Mary from the rest of mankind. Mary is spotless by her own chosen path of holiness. The Mother of God is, as mentioned earlier, the supreme example of synergy.

The Orthodox also differ from the Roman view of Mary's Assumption at the end of her earthly life. The feast is known as the Dormition (Falling asleep) in Orthodoxy. It is part of the Church's *Tradition* that Mary was assumed bodily into heaven, but it is not a dogma. And the point about Dormition is that she *died* first – an event witnessed by most of the apostles. But after three days, her body had gone from her tomb.

The **Orthodox Church** has no equivalent to papal supremacy. The five major Patriarchs together, and the Seven* Ecumenical Councils are the Authority for the whole Orthodox Church, but each Patriarch has ecclesiastical authority within his own jurisdiction. This does *not* include changing doctrine!

The Church is *Trinitarian*. It is the *Body of Christ,* and *Pentecost* is considered to be its birthday.

As the *Body of Christ* the Church includes us sinners *so* the Church must "continue to become what it is." Individual sinners become something different together in the Body of Christ.

In the Church there is no division between the living and the departed. Death cannot sever the "bond of mutual love," so we pray for the dead and we ask *their* prayers.

The Church includes the saints and the angels, but is *One* Church. The saints are a golden chain of those who have gone before us having kept the faith. Icons help bring us closer to that golden chain.

In the stage between death and resurrection on the Last Day we should pray for the departed. We believe these prayers help although we don't understand exactly how. But salvation is only through Christ – "No one comes to the Father except through Me." Jn 14.6

Of the **Last Things**, there are only two ultimate alternatives – Heaven or Hell. Heaven is our reception into the fullness of the presence of God, and Hell is for those who choose to reject God.

Whenever the end comes, it is always *potentially* imminent. The *Parousia* (final revelation) has partly come *now* through the Liturgy and the Church.

————————

*As noted at the beginning of this section, there are two families of Orthodoxy, the Eastern Orthodox Churches (Chalcedonian) and the Oriental Orthodox Churches (non-

Chalcedonian). The former Churches accept all Seven Ecumenical Councils, whereas the latter accept only the first Three.

The 'sticking point' for the Oriental Churches was the definition of the two Natures of Christ (dyophysitism) agreed at the Council of Chalcedon, the Fourth Church Council, the Orientals considering Christ to have one Nature (monophysitism). It is good to note that the two families of Orthodoxy are now seeing that their division has been more one of semantics rather than of doctrine, and it hoped that a unity will evolve that will end this unfortunate rift.

The Celtic Orthodox Church accepts the teaching of all seven councils, whilst acknowledging that only the first three are truly ecumenical, a position which can be described as Pro-Chalcedonian. The Celtic Orthodox Church is *not* monosyphitic.

Typical Celtic monk's cells

The Celtic Orthodox Church:

Origins

Now to look more specifically at the *Celtic* Orthodox Church. Apart from the obvious credentials of the Celtic Church through its boasting countless famous saints – Patrick, Columba, Brigit, Cuthbert, Aidan, to name but a very few – the first thing to say about Celtic Christianity is that it is the original Church of Britain.

Tradition has it that Saint Joseph of Arimathea came to Glastonbury in AD37. I like to believe that this is indeed the case, although it is not provable, and it could be argued that he would have been more likely to have travelled to Cornwall as a trader in tin. But there is no doubt about our next Celtic saint. It *is* clearly documented that Saint Aristobúlus was the first *bishop* in this country in AD63. The Celtic Church held sway here for centuries; until the late seventh century, in fact, when, following the Synod of Whitby in AD664, the established Celtic way was challenged and it began its decline. The key issue for the Synod was to settle the way the date of Pascha/Easter was calculated. But much more was at stake. The more deeply spiritual Celtic way, based on a tradition of monasticism received from the Early Fathers, was at odds with the more rigid and organised Roman way. Thanks to the eloquence of Saint Wilfred over the less articulate proponents of the Celtic position the Roman Church won the day and the Celtic Church began to dwindle until by the 13th century it was all but lost, although some remnants of it remained in isolated pockets long after that, in the remoter parts of Scotland, Wales, Cornwall, Ireland, Brittany (where the present Primate, His Beatitude Metropolitan Marc I, resides), and parts of Northern Spain.

Restoration

The restoration of the Celtic Church began in 1866, by the grace of one inspired man, Bishop Julius (Jules Ferrette), and the intuition of a Metropolitan Bishop of the Syrian Orthodox Church, Mar Boutros (Boutros ibn Salmo Mesko), who later became Patriarch Peter-Ignatius IV. The consecration of Bishop Julius by Mar Boutros was witnessed by the British Consul at Damascus. Bp Julius was given the title of Bishop of Iona and its Dependencies.

Bishop Julius was sent to Britain to form an indigenous Orthodox Church in Western Europe, which was not in any way subject to the Syrian Orthodox Church or the Patriarch of Antioch. The Church, which is autocephalous, was initially known as the Ancient British Church. In 1874 Bp Julius appointed Bp Pelagius I (Richard Williams Morgan) as the first Patriarch of Britain.

In 1944, as a result of merging with other Orthodox/Catholic groups the Church became known as the Catholicate of the West, but this was short-lived (dissolved in 1953), after which the Church was known as the Orthodox Church of the British Isles. (A list of the successive Patriarchs is given at the end of the book.)

Whilst Bishop Georgius I (Hugh George de Willmott Newman) was Patriarch (1945-1979) an interest in rekindling a Celtic spirituality was growing in France. In 1953, Jean-Pierre Danyel (1917-1968 – about whom more will follow) was received into the Glastonbury Patriarchate and ordained priest. He was later consecrated bishop. Bishop Tugdual is important in the development of the Celtic spirituality of the Church. He was canonised by the Celtic Orthodox Church in 1996. A section about him and his teaching follows later.

Meanwhile a small group of spiritual seekers from Southern France, headed by Brother Paul-Eduard de Fournier de Brescia, took monastic vows and were received into the Orthodox Church of the British Isles in 1974. Fr Paul was ordained priest. In 1977 the three monks moved to Saint-Dolay and inhabited the hermitage which had lain abandoned since Bishop Tugdual's death. It was very basic, but gradually the Monastery of the Holy Presence was developed. In 1980 Fr Paul was consecrated bishop by the then Patriarch, Abba Seraphim (William Henry Hugo Newman-Norton), taking the name Mael.

Bishop Tugdual had left copious notebooks (see page 25*ff*) expounding his neo-Celtic spirituality, and, building on these, and his deep devotion to Saint Francis of Assisi, Bishop Mael initiated profound reforms in the Church regaining its (historic) Celtic traditions, Rites and spirit.

Parting of the Ways

In the 1990s, Patriarch Abba Seraphim held discussions with Pope Shenouda III of the Coptic Orthodox Church and he, along with Bishop Mael and Bishop Marc, visited Pope Shenouda, following which, in 1994, most of the UK branch of the Orthodox Church of the British Isles joined the Coptic Orthodox Church, changing its name to the British Orthodox Church. The French branch of the Orthodox Church of the British Isles, considering their mission was better served by remaining as they were, did not follow Abba Seraphim into the Coptic Church. Therefore, on the departure of Abba Seraphim, the Holy Synod of the remaining Church elected Bishop Mael (Paul-Eduard de Fournier de Brescia) as Primate. The Church was renamed the Celtic Orthodox Church. Subsequently, some of the UK clergy who had followed Abba Seraphim into the Coptic Church asked to return to their original Church and were duly received into the Celtic Orthodox Church by Metropolitan Mael. It is deeply sad to record that there was considerable friction between the Celtic Orthodox Church and the British Orthodox Church in the late 1990s.

It is clear that the Celtic Orthodox Church and the British Orthodox Church share a common heritage derived from Jules Ferrette. Consequently, the Celtic Orthodox Community of Saint Gwenn's, Wessex, maintains an amicable relationship with Abba Seraphim and his Church. (In 2015 the British Orthodox Church left the Coptic Church and returned to a state of independence.)

Communion of the Western Orthodox Churches

In 2007 the Celtic Orthodox Church, represented by His Beatitude Metropolitan Mael de Brescia and Bishop Marc Scheerens, the French Orthodox Church, represented by Bishop Vigile and Bishop Martin Laplaud, and the Orthodox Church of the Gauls, represented by Bishop Gregoire Mendez, formed the Communion of the Western Orthodox Churches. The Communion has parishes, monasteries and missions across France, where the Communion was established, and in Belgium, Switzerland, the United Kingdom, Cameroon, Australia, the United States of America, Brazil, and Martinique.

Icon of Saint Tugdual

The Celtic Orthodox Church:

Saint Tugdual and his Teaching

John Peter Danyel was born at Flers in June 1917. Having been abandoned by his parents, he was brought up, un-baptised, by his non-Christian grandmother. We know nothing of his early life, but in his twenties he was in the Army and active in WW2. He was taken prisoner. It was then that he met a Belgian Evangelical pastor and through him found Christ. After the war Tugdual (although that was not yet his name) began to study Christianity. He looked at Protestantism, Catholicism and Orthodoxy. It was within Orthodoxy that he found his home, and he was baptised in May 1949. Later that same year he became a monk.

After trying several communities he was drawn to the Orthodox Church of the British Isles, as the predecessor of our Church was then known. He was ordained priest in March 1953.

In 1955 Tugdual was led by the Holy Spirit to Saint Dolay in Brittany and there, on the edge of a forest, he lived as a holy hermit, at what is now the site of the Monastery of the Holy Presence. In 1956 he was persuaded by the General Chapter of the Order of Saint Columbanus, to become the first bishop of the newly revived *Sainte Église Celtique* (Holy Celtic Church of Brittany.) (Note: he did not *found* the group but was invited to lead it). In 1957 he was consecrated Bishop, taking the name Tugdual.

His life was very simple, austere, and humble; and he was deeply spiritual. Visitors to his hermitage, found in him the "grace of true holiness."

Soon a community began to form around this holy man and it became his ardent desire to found a local church based on the great monastic tradition of the ancient Celtic Church.

Tugdual was never in robust health – which made his extreme asceticism all the more remarkable – and on 11th of August 1968, at the age of 51, he reposed.

Ten years after his death, as he had predicted, a monastic community was founded on the site of his abandoned hermitage (see page 41) under Fr Paul (Paul-Eduard de Fournier de Brescia) who, since 1974, had become part of the Orthodox Church of the British Isles, and thus, Tugdual's legacy is brought into, and becomes an important element of, the Celtic Orthodox Church.

Saint Tugdual was canonised, at that Monastery of the Holy Presence, on Sunday the 11th of August 1996.

His Beatitude Metropolitan Mael said of Tugdual:

"He only preached the Absolute of God, which is the total renouncement of self to God. That means that our love for Christ must become our entire life. This way we will be capable of loving our neighbour as Christ loves each person and each creature here below. Saint Tugdual used to love to remind Bretons of their Christian origins through this sense of the Absolute, which is the very ethos of Celtic

Christianity. All his writings are a vibrant appeal to seize once more this [Celtic] heritage."

Tugdual left almost twenty notebooks containing his thoughts and teachings. Bishop Paul Dupuis explains that Tugdual used an idiosyncratic style of French which makes translation less than straight forward. In the extracts of St Tugdual's writings which follow, I have attempted to make the English translation, previously prepared by the Monastery of Saint Anthony the Great in Egypt, a little more 'accessible.'

Of Wanting and of the Gift

To do God's will it is necessary for the one who aspires to a spiritual life to do their utmost every hour of every day to carry their cross and follow our Lord God and Saviour, Jesus Christ, for without doing this one cannot be His disciple. What does this mean? It means that we must, during every moment of this life that has been consecrated to God and handed over into His keeping, renounce ourselves and mortify our own will, for our will is the root of all pride and the greatest enemy of spirituality. It means that every moment must be a moment of adjusting our own human will to conform to the will of God. In these things we find our own true cross on which the will of the flesh is crucified along with all worldly perversity.

There must be no murmuring of, "I would really like this...or that," "I would really like to be here...or there." How can these things matter? What matters is to know that at any given moment one is accomplishing one's tasks in such a way as would please God; so, what one does is of little significance. All these fluctuating desires are temptations that it is necessary to break upon the rock of faith in Christ the Son of the Living God.

It is not at all necessary to achieve contentment but rather the acceptance of the choices that God, in His uncreated Wisdom, makes for us. Let us, then, do all that He asks with a good heart and live well and in peace wherever He puts us. Let us never forget the golden rule: 'Anything and everything we do has value only in so far as it conforms to the all-holy will of God. Therefore, let us seek to know what is loved by God and to love it in our tum

The touchstone of our spirituality is precisely this: to live less and less according to our own likes and dislikes and more and more to strip the element of personal choice from all we do. Then, certainly and incontestably, our spirituality will take on a strength that will make it both effective and durable, for it will no longer be at the mercy of the fundamental instability of our humanity. Moreover, our spirituality will take on an intrinsic goodness since at the same rate that we progress along the road of self-renunciation our souls will experience a real 'invasion' by the divine which is to say: the more we dispossess ourselves of ourselves the more we come to possess, and be possessed by, God.

God alone is the author of the supernatural order and from this it is easy to understand that He alone can do anything and every thing: all that is needed is His own good will. So, clearly, He is the one we should ask to show us the way to holiness. He never refuses salvation. He may, however, make us search for Him because He wants us to understand that there is a certain path to salvation that is both pleasing to Him and suitable for us, and there is no other way to salvation except along this path. The path to holiness was revealed to us in His Incarnate Word, God-made-man for us. We are all embodied in the full humanity He assumed for us so that he might restore us to the Father. This restoration, to be fully effected, requires nothing but our willing it. If we were to become fully conscious of God's divine plan of redemption and take it into ourself with a real understanding of His special arrangements for each human being, and then in order to adapt to those arrangements we lay aside our own preconceived plans and made up our mind to accept this willingly, then we would be putting our finger on the very heart of holiness.

Steadfastly maintaining this understanding, the soul will find itself ever more and more firmly settled in the Light of Truth, in heavenly peace and harmony under the stable and all-conquering sway of Divine Love.

God is Truth, our Lord God and Saviour Jesus Christ is the way to this Truth and, being God, He is this very Truth come within our reach. It is necessary therefore, that we, in our relation to Him, must also be true. If, for example, we have succumbed to some distraction, or if we have fallen into sinful ways, or if we have been unfaithful to the promptings of grace (and any or all of these may overtake us considering our fallen earthly condition), then we must immediately expose our inner pollution before the face of God's holiness. Straight away we must admit that we have fallen short, we must nakedly expose, as it were, the extent and gravity of the evil we have done. It is necessary that we openly and honestly show our sin to the face of Truth: truth that is regenerative, healing, illuminating and triumphant. This way of behaving has various names: compunction, repentance, regret, propitiation. On this path, that is very humble simple and yet effective, there is no danger of going astray; by it, we attain to a perpetual rehabilitation and what is much more, to the growth that comes with spiritual healing.

So then, the sins we commit because of our fallen nature and tainted birth will not stop God from loving us if we ourselves disapprove of them, regret them and hate them from the bottom of our hearts, for He knows full well our frailty. Moreover, if sin should separate us from God's spotless holiness and put us at variance with it, that would still in no way make any difference to His unchanging love for us.

It is very good for us that we should continually present ourselves before our heavenly Father with all our infirmities, weaknesses and errors and offer ourselves openly for His inspection, as being in truth members of the body of Christ, His only Son, our God. By doing this we may, even in our poverty, make a display of the true virtue of Christ, of His belonging to us and in His death, of His conforming to our human condition. And we know well that the death of the Saviour on Golgotha hill was for universal redemption. It is for us then, in perfect understanding of this mystery, to exploit fully, magnificently, all the possibilities of our situation in as much as we are now members of the body of Jesus Christ.

As we progress along the paths of spirituality, each of us will come to realise for himself or herself that the majority of the difficulties we encounter come from not letting ourselves be guided, led along and inspired by the spirit of Eternal Love; for all perfection, the very essence of becoming like Christ, the core of sanctity, is to be found in the loving accomplishment of the holy will of our God who is blessed forever, Amen.

O that our eyes could see clearly that the truest realm of peace is the will of God and that the sole means of acquiring spiritual calm and equilibrium is to submit entirely to the all-holy will of God.

Whenever trouble comes to us, whenever we lose our interior peace and above all in the middle of difficulties and in the very presence of temptation or face to face with obstacles, let us examine well to see if the root cause of our difficulties be not that we have strayed from our conformity to the divine will to follow our own will, assuage our desires and to live according to our own view of things. By this check on ourselves we can measure the value of our love.

God is so good that He is absolute goodness, far above everything one could say or even imagine; for whatever one says about God falls hopelessly short of His truth. Our God is so good, He who searches out the secrets of our hearts and our innermost parts, that He is always ready, always disposed, always alert to receive from us the least, the tiniest, the most unworthy act, effort, look or sigh of love! For it is Love itself which transfigures all.

This Love is indeed the 'philosophers' stone' for which all the alchemists searched, the stone that will turn base metals to gold, and offer eternal life.
This love that must become ours, this love of which we have so great a need, this love that we want and must give to Him, comes from Him and from Him alone. From Him alone we must continually ask for this love, for it is from Him alone we shall receive it. This love He has placed ready to hand each and every day in the gift of His ineffable Eucharist; for the gift of the holy bread of eternal life and the cup of perpetual salvation is the channel, the sacrament, the guarantee of this love among us, in our midst and deep inside us so long as we turn towards it.

It is in and through our communion of the immaculate body and most precious blood of the Lord that God, in the excess of His love, gives us His love which he has the right to demand of us again but which in fact he begs from us bit by bit like any humble beggar, like any vagabond of the streets, like another poor Lazarus. And we, in our folly, are capable of refusing Him each and every moment.

Unfortunately, too often in our immense ingratitude and in our abominable folly, we totally monopolise the power of loving that God has planted in us, and we hoard it to ourselves; we refuse Him and we bring our sinfulness to a climax by turning our love to worldly things, failing to recognize where our salvation is to be found, or who is our only true benefactor upon whom alone all love must focus. O Blindness, O Folly of mankind; O Goodness, O Patience, O Love both loveable and loving of our God!

O Love, love on, that we may love You! Amen.

An Inexhaustible Treasure

Happily, we have an inexhaustible treasure trove from which we can, at any time, draw freely for all that we lack – and nothing and nobody can ever exhaust its infinite richness. This treasure is our Lord God and Saviour Jesus Christ, the prototype of regenerated, deified, humanity. This is because, on becoming a perfect man at His Incarnation, He did not cease from being the perfect God.

He is our holiness; He is our role-model. At any time we can, by contemplating Him in His mysteries, quench our thirst for truth, inspire ourselves with His bearing and attitudes, and clothe ourselves with His perfection. He is our model in all things and for all things; in humility, in faith, in hope, and in love; in our thoughts, our wills; in affection, tenderness and compassion; in study, work and prayer; in reading and in conversation; in His teaching and in His example; in life, in death, and in His resurrection. He is the model for all our relations with others and for our attitudes towards authority, both spiritual and temporal, towards saints and sinners, angels and demons; towards man and God.

Being our supreme model and matchless prototype, He is also our means of union with God; 'No one comes to the Father, except through Me' (John 14,6). Let us dwell on the idea that our Saviour is present with His disciples on their pilgrimage towards spirituality – a journeying to the Father. 'Going to the Father' is very much part of the Celtic tradition. So, let's consider what 'going to the Father' means in the context of our incorporation in Christ through and in His Church. It is by the out-pouring of the Spirit, that we are 'made over' into Christ, the head, the mysterious body, and in Him become the only Son in whom the Father has put all His trust. The Father's interest in His creation and in His creatures is that He sees in them the Body of His Word, His Christ.

We come to holiness through Jesus Christ our Lord. He is our model, the means of union, and of grace. The Most Holy Spirit implements this presence of Christ in us, and as the Apostle has told us, Christ lives in us by faith.

It is through Christ's holy humanity that the grace, which He earned for us, is given to us, producing in us its perfection and faithfulness.

Consequently, the more we establish, strengthen and reinforce ourselves in this model and prototype, in the Man-God, the more this grace of faithful union will abound and overflow; for where sin abounds, grace will abound more, says Saint Paul (Rom 5, 20). Also, we will become more like God, that is to say, we will the more readily anticipate our entering, now, into the divine perfection.

The grace of Christ comes through our adoption as children of God: adoption that makes us members of the family of God and gives us a part in the heritage of the saints, that is, those sanctified in the Light. Thus, every divine assistance, inspiration, desire or disposition that the Holy Spirit creates in us is for one thing only: to make of us children of God. That is, by the mystery of divine adoption, to transform us into that which the Christ, the Son of the Living God, is by very nature.

Thus, the spiritual life comes down to this: to be so united to the Lord Christ, to be so dominated by His attitudes and behaviour, so filled up with His holiness, that we quite literally become other 'christs' so that, through us, Christ Himself continues His earthly works, and even gives us a foretaste of His resurrection and His glory.

At first sight, all that seems complex and incomprehensible, but it is greatly simplified once we understand that we have only to 'dissolve' ourselves, to lose our soul, will, spirit, affections, life itself, in Christ, for us to become one with Him. It was this experience that lived in Saint Paul when he wrote, "For me to live is Christ." (Phil 1, 21)

What are all our efforts worth? What good will come of all our projects if they are only the expression of our own personalities? It is not so very surprising that we are always colliding with our own humanity, which is but the expression of our self-love with all its consequences – desire for public esteem, pride, nervous sensitivity, extreme touchiness. The only way to break down all these human barriers which retard the growth of the heavenly kingdom within us, is to burn up all the 'I' and all our tenacious ego, burn them up in Christ Himself.

So, let us look upon our great model with clarity of vision; let us look the Christ full in the face. He delivered up His humanity to His divinity as the Word which so subjugated His personal will that, as Saint Paul puts it, "He humbled himself by becoming obedient to death, even death on a cross! Therefore, God exalted Him to the highest place and gave Him the Name that is above every name, that at the Name of Jesus every knee should bow, in heaven and on earth and under the earth." (Phil 2, 8-10)

Of course, there is still pride/love of self with us and it will be with us a long time yet, no doubt, but if only we would consider carefully what an abyss of dangers it is for the soul, and have the courage, energy, readiness and strength to dash its invidious ensnarements against the rock, the cornerstone, that is Christ, then our transforming union with Him will not be slow in coming to perfection.

Given then that we have to undertake a new course of action, a new discipline, we will, no doubt, wish to embrace it wholeheartedly. This is what our Lord spoke of saying, "Watch and pray, yes watch and be on your guard," (Matt 26, 41) so that from the moment natural excitement threatens to take over, you immediately hold it back until you have had recourse to the Model whose divine attitudes and perfections should be considered before undertaking any action. This is the only way to escape from the traps set by the devil and to put our lives back to the way to God, under the direction of His will in the perspective of His grace and glory.

Anyone who is even slightly spiritual will readily understand that if we try to do things on our own no good will come of it. The Lord said, and we must persuade ourselves of its truth, "apart from me you can do nothing." (Jn 15, 5) Therefore, we must keep coming back to God in everything and pray that He will act in us, for then the result will be nothing short of excellent.

Such excellence is simple and easy when we act out of love for God. O, if only we could truly comprehend all the wealth we have in Christ our God, for then we could exploit that wealth to our spiritual advantage, and to that of His Holy Church, to the end that He may be glorified beyond our imagining.

Holy Scripture speaks in many places, of Christ as the Husband. It is a notion that we would do well to take time to consider. Our consecration is nothing other than our engagement or wedding to our heavenly bridegroom. Let us imagine for a moment that we are in the Middle Ages in the times of Lords and their castles.

A young girl from a poor family gets lost in the forest. The wind has blown her hair wild; she has torn her clothes to shreds on the brambles and thorn thickets. Exhausted and hungry she at last drops down on the grass in a clearing. Then a noise is heard in the forest – the galloping of an approaching horse. The Prince is out riding in the forest. He comes to a halt in the clearing where he sees the poor girl and has pity on her. He sees past her rags and discerns that in another setting she would have all the allure of a princess. He lifts her up to ride behind him and takes her to his castle and there he dresses her in the most beautiful of garments and decks her richly with jewels. He installs her in the best room and gives her a harp asking only that she do nothing all the days of her life but sing and be agreeable. This is a short and imperfect presentation of what happens to a sinful soul the day that Christ lifts it up to the palace of His inconceivable Grace.

You will readily understand that from that day forward all the Prince's riches are hers. It is up to her to manifest their value. To do this, two things are necessary — firstly, her soul must surrender itself completely, and secondly, she must identify with the Prince in his every desire.

Spiritually speaking it is the same. This identification of our souls with the good and divine Will derives more from Christ than from us. If we take one step towards Him, He takes a thousand towards us. If we give Him but an insignificant toy from among our many possessions, He will give Himself wholly to us. This is what is meant when it is said that God will never be outdone in generosity!

Thus, the soul, transported to the 'celestial castle,' passes its time gazing with admiration upon its King, expending all its time and energy to please Him in everything out of love for Him, always singing His praise and thanking Him for the many kindnesses He has already shown us and the many benefits He will never cease to shower upon us.

The soul entirely given over to the King, bowing down in submission, occupying itself with divine inspirations, will be richly nourished by them. It is like a good apprentice who applies himself with dedication to his tasks; as he continues to progress steadily in his trade, he acquires, day by day, ever greater skill, dexterity and ease in his work. This will bring contentment and joy to his heart – a profound joy transfiguring his work into the realm of art, and causing him to overflow with an ineffable song of love.

It is this attitude in the artisan that has brought us the beautiful cathedrals that we know and love with all their fine styling. In the exercise of loving, the soul becomes mellow and astute; it acquires a greater inner balance and a serene equanimity which nothing will destroy. So, where sinful nature had imposed disorder, the sovereign order of divine grace comes to reign instead.

In the same way that our poor maiden was taken to the castle and there, in all her finery, learned the habits of aristocratic life, so the soul also, occupied in the service of the divine King, acquires the distinguished character of the people of the court, thereafter irradiating its own newly established inner order.

It is at this moment that the soul, into which the divine graces have deeply penetrated starts to spread abroad its interior riches. The soul is now able to continue zealous for the coming of the Kingdom of God among men! As keeper of an inexhaustible treasure, the new Queen will hereafter be able to assist the King in bountifully distributing his encouragement among the people still living in sadness.

Witnessing to the Resurrection

The Christian in the world must always be the *witness* of the resurrection of his/her Lord. To attest with faith that He was resurrected on the third day, after having endured the atrocious sufferings of his Passion will not suffice: far from it! Just as the Apostle Paul says that if Christ is not resurrected our faith is in vain (1 Cor 15:14) even so, if we who have been buried with Him in the baptism of His death are not resurrected with Him, we do not fulfill the witness to His Resurrection. The apostle defines this resurrection in Christ by Holy Baptism as a newness of Life. Although we are still destined for death, be it soon or be it later, according to the will of God, it is certain that we must *already* behave as mortal Christians as if in the state of the *risen*. This does not mean that in all things we will be able to achieve this ideal, since we must remain for yet awhile in this perishable flesh. It does mean, however, that we must already dwell in Heaven, in the Eternal, through (and transcending) the perishable and the transient. We must, by the means of Christ, without whom we can do nothing: think-anew, want-anew, feel-anew, speak-anew, act-anew.

[*Saint Tugdual creates these neologisms to indicate that we must surpass or go beyond our thoughts, our human will, our emotions, our words and actions, because they are not truth in themselves unless in Christ.*]

Every day we must break more and more with the old man/woman and associate ourselves more and more with the new man/woman created according to God in justice and truth. It is also to deny our way of being, thinking, acting and entering into the way of being, thinking and acting as of Christ, the model and the proto-type, the perpetual complement of our insufficiencies and imperfections by means of permanent communion with its infinite human-divine perfections where our human operations will be deified. To do this is to witness the Resurrection!

The Celtic Orthodox Church:

How our late Primate, His Beatitude Mael, saw it

The importance of His Beatitude Metropolitan Mael's influence in developing the ethos of the Celtic Orthodox Church cannot be sufficiently emphasised. Much can be understood about our Church by reading the following statement, written as a Pastoral Letter when he knew that he was dying.

―――――――――

Beloved sons and daughters in Jesus Christ Our Lord and Saviour, now that I am preparing to go to the Father's House, I feel a need to look back on my forty-one years of serving the Lord in our Mother, the Celtic Orthodox Church.

During the summer and autumn of 2013, along with Bishop Abbot Marc, Bishop Paul and Fathers Nathaneäl and Nil, I have made a broad assessment of all those years.

Twelve points have emerged:

1 Origins *(HB Mael's, not the COC)*

Everything began in 1969 while I was on retreat at the Trappist Orval Abbey in Belgium where I received a definite call to found a community without knowing what kind it would be and even less where we could lay its foundation. Four years later, on January 7,

1973, a small group of us gathered together at Sainte-Geneviève-des-Bois, to the south of Paris, without really knowing where the Holy Spirit would lead us.

In the autumn of 1973 we set up a little chapel in the centre of Montpellier. We prayed there daily. I was consecrated a priest in the Celtic Orthodox Church in August 1974.

A number of defections reduced us to just three brothers! This was a painful period for me, but I never doubted the call that I had received.

By the mercy of God we succeeded in implanting ourselves, in 1977, upon the foundation of our holy Father Tugdual in Brittany. Along with Saint Francis, he constitutes the awakening and restoration of the spirit of our Celtic Fathers.

We lived on Divine Providence. Soon neighbours who had known Saint Tugdual brought us things to eat, and we bartered with the farmers by working with them in exchange for materials or food.

We have endured many tribulations over the years.

Our Church is a local Church of Apostolic origin; it was born on the soil of the British Isles and its mission spread throughout the whole of Europe, preserving a spiritual heritage that is unique in the body of the undivided Church.

My task has been to preserve this heritage, to enrich it and build on the spiritual foundations laid by Saint

Tugdual and Saint Francis of Assisi, our model from our very beginnings in Montpellier

2 The School of Theology

Theological teaching is indispensable. It is the pledge of unity and the safeguard of the Orthodox Faith. Orthodox theology does not differ from one Church to another but each takes on a particular character.

Priests and deacons have the express responsibility of teaching the Faith and transmitting the great spiritual tradition of our Fathers; this must be done in communion with their bishop, who is the protector of the Faith and the Church's spirit. For that, a good theological formation must be the absolute criteria for members of the clergy.

3 The Celtic Orthodox Rite

Every Church has a Rite that it inherited from its Fathers, and several decades were necessary, with the help of liturgical specialists, to restore our Rite. This work is not yet finished. Upon my successor will fall the responsibility of continuing this work, with all the vigilance needed to remain within what is unchanging in the tradition yet updating what is necessary for modern times. Nothing is more contrary to the infinite creativity of the Holy Spirit in Christ than a frozen Rite that belongs to bygone history.

4 Monasteries and Fraternities

Monastic life is central to the Celtic Orthodox tradition. In its spirit the essence of Christian life is monastic, and this same spirit should permeate all our parishes and communities.

5 Unity and Integrity with the Bishop

There is no unity without obedience to the bishop whose ministry it is to safeguard the Faith and unity of the Church. The members of the clergy hold their ministry from the bishop by delegation of a part of his office. A priest or deacon cannot exercise his ministry in the absence of a bishop. There exists a sacramental bond between the bishop and all the members of the clergy, and it is broken if a member of the clergy is no longer in obedience.

6 Ecumenism

Ecumenism is at the heart of our spirit. By nature the Church is divine and indivisible, and we must consider that nothing can divide it because the Body of Christ cannot be divided. The quest for the visible unity of all the Churches must form part of our personal, ecclesial life.

The coexistence of various Orthodox Churches, which stem from immigration and have taken root in the culture of our countries, forms part of a divine plan whose shape remains unknown to us. We do not know how the Holy Spirit will guide us toward visible unity, but it is authentic life in Christ—and only that—which will allow for the unity of the Church.

7 Inter-religious Dialogue

Christians have changed their outlook towards other religions since the great interreligious gathering of Assisi in 1986.

Let us not be afraid of opening ourselves up to the brother who comes from another Faith. Let us welcome him as Christ welcomed everyone who came to Him. It is not a matter of converting people to a doctrine, but of revealing Christ in the heart of each person.

8 Gospel and Faith

Saint Francis of Assisi says: "The Rule of life of the Friars consists in living the Holy Gospel." The great monastic tradition and the writings of the Fathers have, in act and in writing, fully given the meaning of the Word of God. All watering down of the Faith comes from a worldly interpretation of the Gospel. The worries of the world stifle the voice of the Holy Spirit. The Faith is a gift of God that grows as we renounce the illusions of the world.

9 Charity

Recently Pope Francis said, "Love of neighbour is such a fundamental attitude that the relationship between man and God cannot be sincere if he does not make peace with his neighbour."

And Saint Tugdual taught that:
"Celtic Christianity's true tone is summed up by these words:
Do good.
Bless always.
Pray for all."

So, let us be apostles of love, even at the cost of our life, as the Lord showed us on the Cross. The Cross brings about the Salvation of the world, for it is Love in the Absolute, forever defeating the hell of darkness.

10 Love of Creation and Bioethics

You know what place the love and protection of creation occupies in our Church. The tragedy of the destruction of our environment and the serious consequences that are descending upon the world urgently require that we all work in tandem with each other.

Eco-spirituality and questions of bioethics form an integral part of Christian theology and draw their source from the Orthodox Faith. Theological ethics has become a fundamental matter.

11 Holy Presence Monastery

The Holy Presence Monastery is the historical foundation of the restoration of the Celtic Orthodox Church in France, as well as the restoration of the monastic spirituality that is the very spirit of the entire Orthodox tradition. In this place our holy Father Tugdual received the absolute certainty that his work would not perish and that it would become a tree whose branches would rise up to heaven.
Many years ago, long after we had dedicated the cathedral to Our Lady of the Sign, I received the assurance that the Mother of God wanted a sanctuary at Holy Presence.

We have received much and will still receive an abundance of grace so long as we remain true to the Faith and the spirit of our Fathers.

12 Communion of the Western Orthodox Churches

There exist several ancient Western Christian traditions. In 2007 we participated in the creation of the Communion of Western Orthodox Churches, enabling three Orthodox Churches to unite, sharing a spirituality based on the same Absolute of God, the same liturgical cycle and numerous common liturgical sources. The bishops of this Communion form a permanent active college in order to make our respective Churches move forward toward a greater harmonization of our customs and traditions, and to allow the clergy and faithful to be fully received in each of the sister Churches.

This pastoral letter is my testament. May all of you receive it as the fruit of an entire life dedicated to God and of a heritage received from my Fathers and transmitted to you in order that the Will of God may be fulfilled!

I invoke the Holy Trinity to bless you, my beloved sons and daughters, that you might all remain united in the same spirit, the same Faith and an unfailing charity as the Lord asks: "Love one another as I have loved you."

Celtic Spirituality

But what of Celtic Spirituality itself. How does it nourish us in our Christian pilgrimage today? Here are a few key thoughts.

Firstly, we should never look at the beauty of Creation without seeing God within it and giving Him thanks. In the Gospel we learn how God feeds the birds of the air and adorns the fields in glorious array. These are His creatures and He cares for them. Thus should we too love and care for our environment. (See earlier reference to God's immanence.)

Secondly, we should always remember that God makes every place Holy for us if we will allow him. Our churches are special, and so are many holy sites, but God is behind us, before us, within us, where*ever* we are, and we should learn to meet Him there, wherever it may be. That said, the Celts speak of 'thin' places. These are places where the veil between heaven and earth seems particularly thin and communion with God seems to come more readily.

Thirdly, in true Celtic fashion we might begin every day with a caim, prayer – pronounced 'kyme.' We encircle ourselves, describing a circle in the air with our right hand held high, and make our prayer to God – for example:

Circle me, Lord: Protect me and keep danger afar.

Circle me, Lord: Give me hope and banish doubt.

Circle me, Lord: Be my Light and keep darkness afar.

Circle me, Lord: Give me peace within and keep evil without.

And at the end of every day (having first had a time of both penitence and thanksgiving) we commend ourselves and our loved ones to God's protection with typical Celtic prayers such as:

Calm me, O Lord, as You stilled the storm.
Still me, O Lord, and keep me from harm.
Let all the tumult within me cease.
Enfold me, O Lord, in Your peace.

Christ God Who sinned not, O Christ of wounds,
I place my soul and body under Your protection this night.

And fourthly, it is the Celtic way to offer God's blessing to everyone we meet – a typical Celtic greeting *cum* blessing is:

May all that is good rise up to meet you, and may all that is evil fall from your path.

The Celtic Cross

Most people are aware that the Celtic Church has its own distinctive cross. The design is often attributed to Saint Patrick.

Basically, it is the cross of Christ's sacrifice, with the addition of a circle. It's probable that the circle was borrowed from our Druid forebears, bringing new and deeper meaning to the circle of the sun and the circle of eternity. So the Celtic cross shews how Christ is the centre, holding all the fullness of Life and Creation in a single glorious piece.

The Celts being very artistic, Celtic crosses are frequently elaborately decorated, all to the Glory of God.

The Celtic Church was part of the one undivided Early Church, which was, of course, Orthodox until, in the West, the Roman Catholic Church broke away in 1054, although, as mentioned earlier, Rome's influence had been felt in the West some time before their formal break with Orthodoxy.

Consequently, the original, and the present, Celtic Church has more in common with the Orthodox Tradition than with Roman Catholicism. But we are *Western* Orthodox, and not part of the Eastern Orthodox families of the Church although our Faith is one.

However, we are rather more ecumenical than either the Orthodox or the Roman Church. We welcome to our altars all who are baptised and communicant members of a Church which accepts the Nicene Creed, *and* – this is very important to us – who believe Christ to be truly present in the consecrated bread and wine which become the body and blood of Him Who gave Himself for our salvation.

Christ is greater than the denominational boundaries we have sadly and disgracefully set for Him.

Celtic worship tends be somewhat longer than modern Christians are used to. That is because, to the early Celtic Christians, their Faith was the very centre of their lives. Nothing was more important to them.

Today I fear we all too easily 'side-line' God. We feel our church services must be shorter so that we can get home and prepare the lunch or get out onto the golf course, or a whole host of other things that excite us more than God. And that's just those of us who come to church at all. For the majority of people, the garden or the Sunday paper, or whatever, wins completely.

To enter into the mystery and awe of true Celtic worship, or any Orthodox worship for that matter, we need a different 'mind-set.' We need to give ourselves over entirely to the joy of praising God, and not allow fretting about getting home to do something else get in the way. Nothing is more important than God.

Celtic worship and spirituality, as already avowed, is very Trinitarian. In particular think of the great hymn attributed to Saint Patrick; *I bind unto myself today, the strong name of the Trinity.* And Saint Patrick, we believe, was the first to use the three lobes of the one clover leaf to illustrate in simple terms the concept of the Triune God.

Other things to note will include the fact that we stand for worship and that all our prayers are sung. We make frequent use of the sign of the cross. We do this in a special way. We join our first two fingers of our right hand to our thumb, representing the Trinity, and close our second two fingers into the palm, representing the two Natures of Christ. And the cross is traced from head to breast, then right shoulder to left shoulder. This latter, which differs from the Latin Western tradition, emphasises that Christ sits at the right hand of the Father.

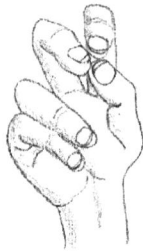

The right hand is held thus when making the sign of the cross.

The sign of the cross is made to focus our minds, through a manual act, at certain important moments in prayer. Most typically it is used when we say, "Lord, have mercy," and when "Father, Son, and Holy Spirit" occurs in or at the end of a prayer.

The Celtic Orthodox, as with all Orthodox, stress the importance of prayerful preparation before receiving communion, and thanksgiving prayers are said after communion. Fasting before communion is required. It is normal to abstain from all food from bedtime the day before, or, if the Liturgy is in the evening, then as near as possible to six hours is recommended, but certainly not less than four hours. Drinking water is permitted. However, if there are medical reasons why a person needs to eat, then the fasting rules may be relaxed. Assurance on this is usually sought from the parish priest.

We also observe a fasting diet on Fridays* (except in Paschaltide), during Advent, and during Lent. We abstain from animal products and alcohol.

*Optionally, also Wednesdays.

Lindisfarne today

Celtic Reflections

To round off this little introduction to Celtic Orthodoxy and Spirituality I am going to offer three short Reflections on Celtic themes, and then a trio of Celtic prayer poems.

Saint Patrick – Christ around us

Patrick was born in England – some think in Glastonbury, but probably Cumbria – around AD390, into a Christian family; his grandfather a priest, and his father a deacon. As a teenager he was captured and taken as a slave to Ireland where he was set to tend animals out on the hills, leaving him plenty of peace to reflect on God. After six years he escaped and made his way to the coast to find a ship to take him home to England. Back here he became a priest, and God called him to return to Ireland as a missionary. The rest, as they say, is history.

He is thought to have returned once again to England in AD443 and gone to Glastonbury where he found twelve anchorites. He formed them into a community. Some even say he stayed at Glastonbury until he died, but most think he returned to Ireland where he died somewhere between 460 and 487 – there are conflicting accounts – but the burial location is unknown. Interesting as there are several authenticated fragments of his relics!

The famous Lorica or Breastplate of Saint Patrick, also known as The Deer's Cry, may or may not be wholly by him – the oldest manuscript of it dates from the eighth century – but it would certainly be representative of his typically Celtic form of prayer, surrounding himself with the power of God to protect himself from evil.

I have made my own version of part of the Lorica which I frequently use as an alternative to praying the Jesus Prayer. It is, however, quite effective simply to repeat, "Christ around me; Christ within me." The important thing is to keep one's attention fixed on Christ around us.

You can say this aloud, or silently, but it should be slow and meditative, almost hypnotic, as you rest in Christ's presence.

Christ before me, Christ behind me,

Christ above me, Christ beneath me.

Christ to my right, Christ to my left,

Christ around me, Christ within me.

Christ to guide me, Christ to guard me,

Christ to heal me, Christ to love me.

Saint Kevin's Glendalough Monastery

Saint Kevin – Stillness and Nature

Saint Kevin was born in Ireland around 498, very possibly of a noble family. From the age of seven he was educated by Saint Petroc of Cornwall who travelled to Ireland around that time. Kevin lived with a monastic community until he was twelve. Later he studied for the priesthood, and after his ordination moved Glendalough – Glen of the two lakes – a remote area, where he lived as a hermit.

He lived close to Nature with birds and animals as his friends. His reputation as a holy and wise man grew, and others joined him, and so a monastery was established at Glendalough.

Many legends surround the life of Saint Kevin, the most enduring being about a blackbird. It is said that Kevin stood in prayer, hands outstretched, so still and for so long that a blackbird built its nest in the palm of his hand. Eggs were laid, incubated, and the baby birds fed until they were able to fly away – only *then* did Saint Kevin move!

There are several embellishments to this legend – small cell, hand out of window; up to his waist in the lake; during Lent, and birds flew in time for Kevin to get to church for Easter, and so on.

This is not to be taken literally, but such a story would only have come about because Saint Kevin obviously spent *extremely* long periods in prayer.

So, let us learn from this to reflect on how much time we make to spend in prayer with God. And also on how much we notice, reflect on, and thank God for, the world around us.

A Reflection on Celtic Beauty

The Celtic Church abounded in art. Perhaps the greatest examples are the fantastic illuminated manuscripts such as the Lindisfarne Gospels. These glorious works were all produced to the Glory of God. So too were the poetry and prayers of the Celtic Christians. I have no doubt that their music too would have been a praiseworthy offering, but sadly, we have no idea of what it sounded like, beyond a shrewd guess that the Traditional Irish and Scottish folk music that has come down to us probably gives us *some* sort of clue. An un-named monk wrote in the margin of his page: "How well I write in the greenwood!" Maybe the animal heads in his illuminations are those of the shy, wild creatures who peeped out of the bushes to watch the silent monk at work!

We too should reflect on beauty. Indeed there is much around us that is less than beautiful, but let's try to focus on finding beauty in what surrounds us. Rejoice in the lovely things that God has inspired man to create, but above all look for the beauty of God's own creation – and not just look, but listen. Let yourself be inspired.

In sunlight see the brightness of Christ's light.

In rain see the life-giving water we need to sustain us and the earth.

In the call of the birds hear the cherubim and seraphim praising God.

In the wideness of the sky see the immensity of God.

In a tiny insect see the minuteness of God's attention to detail.

Iona today

To conclude, here are some Celtic and neo-Celtic
Prayer Poems

Deep peace of the running wave to you,
Deep peace of the flowing air to you,
Deep peace of the quiet earth to you,
Deep peace of the shining stars to you,
Deep peace of Christ the Son to you.

Come I this day to the Father,
Come I this day to the Son,
Come I to the Holy Spirit powerful;
Come I this day with God,
Come I this day with Christ,
Come I with the Spirit of kindly balm

God, and Spirit, and Jesus,
From the crown of my head
To the soles of my feet;
Come I with my reputation,
Come I with my testimony,
Come I to You, Jesu;
Jesu, shelter me.

Praise God in His Holiness,
Praise Him in the firmament of His Power,
Tumbling brooks, silver, whisper praises to His Name.

Praise God mighty oak,
Praise Him in the elm, grandeur,
Sighing pines breath praises through chill air.

Praise God jagged heights,
Praise Him in the wild and moorland wastes,
Curlews crying, haunting, lonesome, praise His Name.

Praise God bracken fronds,
Praise Him in the lush green grass,
Wind blow, corn sway, heather sing His praise.

Praise God sky and clouds,
Praise Him in the wind blown leaves rustle,
Sheep bleat, bird sing, Praise His Name.

Praise God raging sea,
Praise Him in the dashing spray, coral,
Screaming gull, blue, green, and stormy grey; praise.

Praise God thousand thing,
Praise Him in the earth and sea,
Heaven, mighty oak, wind blow, curlew, praise His Name.

Bishops of the Western Orthodox Communion c2007

APPENDIX – Patriarchs/Primates

The following are the Patriarchs of Britain and Primates of the Celtic Orthodox Church in succession:

[Bishop Julius (Jules Ferrette) was *de facto* head of the Church from 1866 until the appointment of the first Patriarch]

Mar Pelagius I (Richard Williams Morgan), consecrated in 1874 by Bishop Julius (Jules Ferrete). Tenure (Patriarch) 1874-1889.

Mar Theophilus I (Charles Isaac Stevens), consecrated in 1879 by Mar Pelagius. Tenure (Patriarch) 1889-1917.

Mar Jacobus I Antipas (James Martin), consecrated in November 1890 by Leon Chechemian who was himself consecrated in May 1890 by Mar Theophilus (and Bishop Alfred Spencer Richardson). Tenure (Patriarch) 1917-1919.

Mar Andries I (Andrew Charles Albert McLaglan), consecrated in 1897 by Leon Chechemian and Mar Jacobus I Antipas. Tenure (Patriarch) 1919-1928.
Mar Jacobus II (Herbert James Monzani-Heard), consecrated in 1922 by Mar Andries I. Tenure (Patriarch) 1928-1945.

Mar Georgius I (Hugh George de Willmott Newman), consecrated in 1944 by Mar Basilius (William Bernard Crow) on behalf of Mar John Emmanuel (Arthur Wolfort Brooks). Mar Basilius had himself been consecrated in 1943 by Mar Jacobus II. Tenure (Patriarch) 1945-1979.

Abba Seraphim I (William Henry Hugo Newman-Norton), consecrated in 1977 by his cousin Mar Georgius, assisted by two other bishops, Bishop Smethurst and Bishop Raoult. Tenure (Patriarch) 1979-1994.

Metropolitan Mael I (Paul-Eduard de Fournier de Brescia) consecrated in 1980 by Mar Seraphim. Tenure (Primate) 1994-2014.

Metropolitan Marc I (Jean-Claude Scheerens), consecrated in 1998 by Metropolitan Mael. Tenure (Primate) 2014 to the present.

Suggested Further Reading

The Orthodox Church: Metropolitan Kallistos Ware

The Orthodox Way: Metropolitan Kallistos Ware

Celtic Christianity: Timothy Joyce OSB

The Celtic Way of Prayer   Esther de Waal

Celtic Christian Spirituality: Mary C Earle

The Celtic Heart   Pat Robson

The Edge of Glory   David Adam

Eternal Echoes   John O'Donohue

Early Celtic Christianity: Brendan Lehane

Useful websites

Celtic Orthodox Church – in French
www.orthodoxie-celtique.org

Communion of Western Orthodox Churches – in French
www.orthodoxie-occidentale.org

Community of St Gwenn's, UK
www.stgwenns.org

Other Celtic Orthodox Books Published by Lamorna Publications (Compiled/edited by Fr Leonard Hollands)

The St Gwenn's Celtic Orthodox Prayer Book

The St Gwenn's Celtic Orthodox Daily Office Book

The Divine Liturgy of the Celtic Orthodox Church

The St Gwenn Celtic Orthodox Services for Lent, Holy Week and Pascha

The Celtic Orthodox Calendar (yearly)

The Little Celtic Prayer Book